GRAPHIC BIOGRAPHIES

PATRICK HENRY
Liberty or Death

by Jason Glaser
illustrated by Peter McDonnell

Consultant:

Wayne Bodle, PhD
Assistant Professor of History
Indiana University of Pennsylvania

Capstone
press

Mankato, Minnesota

Graphic Library is published by Capstone Press,
151 Good Counsel Drive, P.O. Box 669, Mankato, Minnesota 56002.
www.capstonepress.com

1 2 3 4 5 6 10 09 08 07 06 05

Library of Congress Cataloging-in-Publication Data
Glaser, Jason.
    Patrick Henry: liberty or death / by Jason Glaser; illustrated by Peter McDonnell.
    p. cm.—(Graphic library. Graphic biographies)
    Summary: "In graphic novel format, tells the life story of Patrick Henry, who is known as the
'Voice of the American Revolution.'"—Provided by publisher.
    Includes bibliographical references and index.
    ISBN 0-7368-4970-X (hardcover)
    1. Henry, Patrick, 1736–1799—Juvenile literature. 2. Legislators—United States—
Biography—Juvenile literature. 3. United States. Continental Congress—Biography—Juvenile
literature. 4. Virginia—Politics and government—1775–1783—Juvenile literature. 5. United
States—Politics and government—1775–1783—Juvenile literature. I. McDonnell, Peter, ill. II.
Title. III. Series.
E302.6.H5G59 2006
973.3'092—dc22   2005004011

Art and Editorial Direction
Jason Knudson and Blake A. Hoena

Designers
Bob Lentz and Linda Clavel

Editor
Christopher Harbo

Editor's note: Direct quotations from primary sources are indicated by a yellow background.

Direct quotations appear on the following pages:
Pages 12, 14 (right), from *Patrick Henry: Patriot in the Making* by Robert Douthat Meade
    (Philadelphia: J. B. Lippincott Company, 1957).
Page 14 (left), from *Patrick Henry and His World* by George F. Willison (Garden City, N.Y.:
    Doubleday and Company, 1969).
Pages 15, 27, from *Patrick Henry: Practical Revolutionary* by Robert Douthat Meade
    (Philadelphia: J. B. Lippincott Company, 1969).
Page 25, from *Patrick Henry* by Moses Coit Tyler (Ithaca, N.Y.: Great Seal Books, 1962).

TABLE OF CONTENTS

CHAPTER 1

FINDING HIS PATH

When Patrick Henry was born in Hanover County in 1736, Virginia was a British colony.

Patrick's parents wanted their son to be educated. But he was much more interested in other things.

You missed school again, Patrick.

Say, is that your brother's rifle?

It's mine now. I talked him into a trade.

When Patrick was 10, his father, John, stopped sending him to school. Patrick's father taught him at home.

Translate this Latin into English.

We never worked this hard at school!

Nihil enim umquam

How would you know? You seldom showed up.

When Patrick was 15, his parents decided he should get a job.

You won't study, and you don't like farming. What will you do for a living?

I could work at a store. I can get people to buy lots of supplies.

I bet you would make a good store clerk. I will give you and your brother money to start a store.

At age 18, Patrick married Sarah Shelton. Their parents gave the young couple cattle, slaves, and a 300-acre plantation called Pine Slash.

CHAPTER 2

VOICE OF LIBERTY

In Virginia, British law said church ministers would be paid in tobacco. But in 1758, the tobacco harvest was poor. Virginia lawmakers passed a law saying ministers would be paid two pennies for each pound of tobacco they usually received. Ministers were outraged.

I could sell the tobacco owed me for more than two pennies a pound.

But Uncle, people must have freedom to change laws when times are tough.

You may think so, but Great Britain has rejected Virginia's two-penny law.

In the early 1760s, some ministers sued to get more money for their 1758 wages.

Meanwhile, colonists were still frustrated with British taxes. They especially hated the tax on tea. On December 17, 1773, they tossed a shipload of tea leaves into Boston Harbor. The British were furious about the Boston Tea Party.

What the colonists did is unforgivable. They destroyed British property!

The town of Boston ought to be knocked about the ears and destroyed!

Great Britain passed laws to punish the colonies.

In September 1774, the colonies held the First Continental Congress in Philadelphia to decide what actions to take against Great Britain. Patric traveled with George Washington to the meeting.

Tobacco is Virginia's weapon. Great Britain will listen if we stop sending tobacco.

If the colonies don't unite, even that weapon is useless.

At the meeting, delegates discussed America's rights and ways to limit Parliament's power. Patrick called for the colonies to work together.

The differences between our people are no more.

I am not a Virginian, but an American.

CHAPTER 3

WARTIME LEADER

Great Britain feared a revolution. The British sent soldiers to Massachusetts to take the ammunition and gunpowder the colonists had hidden there. On April 19, 1775, colonists in Concord and Lexington defended themselves against British troops. The Revolutionary War had begun.

Attack!

Fire at will!

Patrick faced news of the revolution alone. Sarah had died earlier that year. But he soon rose above his grief to act for his country.

16

Patrick's second term was followed by a third term in 1778. As governor, he worked with lawmakers to supply Virginia's military during the war.

The army needs more clothing. Have the county officers collect shoes and gloves for each soldier raised in their county.

For four years, the war was fought north and south of Virginia. In May 1779, a fleet of British ships sailed into Chesapeake Bay on Virginia's coast. The British destroyed several ships at Portsmouth and raided supplies from the town of Suffolk.

Patrick sent orders to Virginia's military officers and county lieutenants.

Ride quickly.

The county lieutenants must have their militias ready to fight in case the British invade Virginia.

Yes, sir!

Fortunately, the British fleet did not launch an attack into Virginia. After two weeks of raids, the fleet sailed away.

One month later, Patrick's third term as governor ended. Patrick moved his family to Henry County. He hoped the war wouldn't reach that far inland.

This is Leatherwood, our new home.

Patrick didn't stay at Leatherwood long. Soon, he was elected to the House of Delegates. The House was part of Virginia's new legislature. Leaving his family behind, Patrick moved to Richmond to help guide Virginia through the last years of war.

I propose sending someone to Congress to explain the condition of Virginia.

I agree!

Excellent idea!

In early 1781, the British army finally invaded Virginia. Patrick and the other members of the General Assembly fled Richmond to avoid capture.

How far west do you think we must go to escape the British?

With luck, the town of Staunton on the other side of these mountains will be far enough.

CHAPTER 4

FINAL YEARS OF SERVICE

In the fall of 1784, the General Assembly elected Patrick governor of Virginia again.

Do you swear to honestly perform the duties of Governor of Virginia?

I do.

Patrick was elected again the next year. As governor, he worked to strengthen Virginia's economy after years of war. In the meantime, the new U.S. government was taking shape.

After five terms as governor, Patrick, now 51 years old, returned to his law practice.

I'm still amazed at your arguments, Patrick.

Sir, George Washington sends this message.

This must be a copy of the proposed U.S. Constitution.

In June 1788, a state convention was held to decide if Virginia would accept or reject the new U.S. Constitution. Patrick argued against ratifying the Constitution.

This document doesn't list the rights of the people.

The necessity of a Bill of Rights appears to me to be greater in this government than ever it was in any government before.

After three weeks of debate, the delegates cast their votes. Virginia accepted the Constitution by only 10 votes.

In 1789, George Washington was elected the nation's first president. While in office, he offered Patrick several jobs. Patrick declined the offers. He decided to retire.

Patrick, it's a beautiful day. Why don't you take the grandchildren for a walk along the river?

That's a great idea!

Patrick lost the fight. But his beliefs were held by many others. In 1789, Congress passed 10 amendments to the Constitution. These amendments became known as the Bill of Rights.

Patrick spent time with his large family on an estate called Red Hill.

Meanwhile, the new nation struggled to build strong state and national governments. In 1799, George Washington asked Patrick to run for state legislature. Patrick agreed and gave a single campaign speech.

I will work to soothe the hard feelings tearing our legislature apart.

United we stand, divided we fall. Let us not split into factions which must destroy that union upon which our existence hangs.

Patrick won the election, but he never took office. He died at home on June 6, 1799. The voice of an American patriot fell silent, but his words lived on. With his cry for "liberty or death," Patrick had moved a country to action and changed the course of American history.

PATRICK HENRY
1736-1799
His Fame His Best Epitaph

PATRICK HENRY

- Patrick Henry was born May 29, 1736, in Hanover County, Virginia. He died June 6, 1799, at the age of 63.

- With Patrick's help, Kentucky became a county of Virginia in 1776. It became its own state in 1792.

- Patrick became a colonel of Virginia's First Regiment and commander of Virginia's regular forces in August 1775. His soldiers liked him, but some members of Virginia's government didn't think he had enough military experience. As a result, his regiment wasn't given many missions. After five months in the military, Patrick resigned.

- Patrick had only been in the House of Burgesses for nine days before he presented his Stamp Act Resolutions.

- Patrick had 17 children. He had six children with his first wife, Sarah, and 11 with his second wife, Dorothea.

- Patrick helped to start Hampden Sydney College in Virginia. He believed that it was the duty of the state to educate its citizens.

Patrick fought hard for a Bill of Rights to be added to the U.S. Constitution. In 1789, 10 amendments, known as the Bill of Rights, were added to the Constitution. One of these amendments granted all citizens the rights of freedom of religion, speech, and the press.

Patrick turned down several job offers after he retired to Red Hill. These jobs included Chief Justice of the Supreme Court, Secretary of State, and minister to Spain and to France.

With Patrick's will, his family found a copy of his Stamp Act Resolutions. On the back was written "Reader! Whoever thou art, remember this . . . practice virtue thyself, and encourage it in others."

GLOSSARY

damages (DAM-ij-es)—money given to people by a court of law to make up for an injury or a loss they have suffered

parliament (PAR-luh-muhnt)—the governing body that makes the laws in Britain

pound (POUND)—a unit of money used in England and several other countries; also a unit of weight equal to 16 ounces.

resolution (rez-uh-LOO-shuhn)—a formal statement of an opinion or decision

treason (TREE-zuhn)—betraying one's country, especially by helping the enemy or plotting to overthrow the government

tyrant (TYE-ruhnt)—someone who rules other people in a cruel or unjust way

INTERNET SITES

FactHound offers a safe, fun way to find Internet sites related to this book. All of the sites on FactHound have been researched by our staff.

Here's how:

1. *Visit www.facthound.com*
2. Type in this special code **073684970X** for age-appropriate sites. Or enter a search word related to this book for a more general search.
3. Click on the **Fetch It** button.

FactHound will fetch the best sites for you!

READ MORE

Kukla, Amy, and Jon Kukla. *Patrick Henry: Voice of the Revolution.* The Library of American Lives and Times. New York: PowerKids Press, 2002.

Marquette, Scott. *Revolutionary War.* America at War. Vero Beach, Fla.: Rourke, 2003.

McPherson, Stephanie Sammartino. *Liberty or Death: A Story about Patrick Henry.* A Creative Minds Biography. Minneapolis: Carolrhoda Books, 2003.

Williams, Jean Kinney. *The U.S. Constitution.* We the People. Minneapolis: Compass Point Books, 2004.

BIBLIOGRAPHY

Meade, Robert Douthat. *Patrick Henry: Patriot in the Making.* Philadelphia: J. B. Lippincott, 1957.

Meade, Robert Douthat. *Patrick Henry: Practical Revolutionary.* Philadelphia: J. B. Lippincott, 1969.

Tyler, Moses Coit. *Patrick Henry.* Ithaca, N.Y.: Great Seal Books, 1962.

Willison, George F. *Patrick Henry and His World.* Garden City, N.Y.: Doubleday, 1969.

INDEX